THE DANCE OF LIFE

OUT OF SILENCE

Script By:

Margaret Doak

Photographs By:

James (Jim) Doak

and others where stated

Pen Press

First published in Great Britain

All paper used in the printing of this book has been made from wood grown in managed, sustainable forests.

ISBN13: 978-1-78003-306-8

Printed and bound in the UK
Pen Press is an imprint of
Indepenpress Publishing Limited
25 Eastern Place
Brighton
BN2 1GJ

A catalogue record of this book is available from
the British Library

Cover design by Jacqueline Abromeit

I dedicate this book

To my brother Jim whose photography so often captured aspects of the Creation he loved so much and inspired me to write these reflections.

and

To our parents who instilled such love in us.

ERRATA

- in Foreword , line 7 first paragraph :
  "the" animal,not "this" ;
  line 5 second paragraph:
  "meditations", not "mediations"

- page 14 : two photos should be reversed,
  caption ok

- page 70: the first photo should read
  "Ely Cathedral" , Cambridgeshire;
  photo 2 & 3 :Spanish Church
  Architecture

- page 71: last line second paragraph should
  read "Canterbury" , not Sens

- page 105 , lines 5 & 6 ,second paragraph
  should omit : "horse power and"

Acknowledgements

My thanks are due to the following publishers, copyright owners and authors for permission to use the following extracts and quotations.

Cambridge University Press
1) "Extracts from the Authorised Version of the Bible (The King James Bible), the rights in which are vested in the Crown, are reproduced by permission of the Crown's Patentee, Cambridge University Press."

2) "Extracts from The Book of Common Prayer, the rights in which are vested in the Crown, are reproduced by permission of the Crown's Patentee, Cambridge University Press."

Everyman who have granted me free permission to quote four lines from John Keats' poem 'Ode to Autumn' from *Poems – John Keats* in the Everyman Edition of 1944.

Harper Collins for use of four verses from the Revised Standard Version and "Reprinted by permission of Harper Collins Publishing Ltd © 1946-52. Revised 1971. Division of Christian Education of the National Council of Churches of Christ in the United States of America."

Hodder and Stoughton who have granted me free permission to quote from the New International Version of the Bible, first published in 1978 and this edition 1980, New York Bible Society.

Scripture quotations [marked NIV] taken from the Holy Bible, New International Version Anglicised. Copyright © 1979, 1984, 2011 Biblica, formerly International Bible Society – used by permission of Hodder and Stoughton Publishers, an Hachette UK Company. All rights reserved: "NIV" is a registered trademark of Biblica UK trademark number 1448790.

Oxford University Press
1) For use of the line "Like wheat that springeth green" as a chapter heading. Copyright acknowledgement. From "Now the green blade riseth" by J MC Crum (1878-1958) [altered]. Extract reproduced by permission of Oxford University Press. All rights reserved. IP Number 5002903.

2) For one line "Skilled at the plane and the lathe". Copyright acknowledgement. From "Lord of all Hopefulness" words by Jan Struther (1901-53) from

CONTENTS

III THE FOUR SEASONS

A WINTER
1 Out of Silence
2 "In the Bleak Mid-Winter" - Birth

B SPRING
1 "Like Wheat that Springeth Green"
2 Easter - "The Queen of Seasons Bright"

C SUMMER
1 Halcyon Days
2 The First Fruits of Harvest

D AUTUMN
1 "Season of Mists and Mellow Fruitfulness"
2 The Final Reaping

IV PRAYER AND WORSHIP

1 Worship in Nature
2 Church and Congregation
3 The Breaking of Bread – The Eucharist
4 Aids to Worship
5 Holy Places
6 Monasticism
7 Private Prayer

V MAN'S USE OF NATURAL RESOURCES

1 Forestry
2 Farming
3 Fishing

ARCHBISHOP
OF CANTERBURY

FOREWORD
for
Margaret Doak's *The Dance of Life: Out of Silence*

Do we really think of ourselves as part of creation? The obvious
answer might be yes; but in fact, we are deeply prone to behave as
though humans are beings of another order from the environment in
which they exist. We forget the patterns of dependence that sustain
our lives. We forget how much we owe to the landscapes we can
see, the vegetable life surrounding us and the very varied relations
we have with this animal word; we don't realise how much we learn
unconsciously from all this.

The belief that God made human beings as the crown of creation
or the stewards or even the priests of creation does not mean that
they are somehow walled off from the rest of life. On the contrary,
it means that we do not have meaning as humans without these
relationships with all that lies around us. In these mediations,
Margaret Doak offers us ways of reconnecting with the real world
of landscape and plant life and the animal creation as a means of
becoming more human. In simple but evocative words and beautiful
images, she encourages us into deeper prayer and understanding of
our faith, leading us from the direct contemplation of the natural
world towards reflection on our creative use of that world and the
supreme use of creativity in the symbols and sacraments of Christian
practice. This is an ideal resource for study in parishes and other
Christian groups and I am delighted to recommend it.

+ Rowan Cantuar

Lambeth Palace
Pentecost 2011

Lambeth Palace, London SE1 7JU

INTRODUCTION & ACKNOWLEDGEMENTS

DANCE is of the essence of life and as it features in the Old Testament it suggests that it was very much part of religious experience as in other religions and has once again entered modern Christian worship. Dance is a way of expressing one's unity and solidarity with all Creation and therefore with the Creator Himself Who entered our world in human form out of the silence of Heaven. Silence is not just the absence of noise. Rather it is an entering into the state of Heaven where all is calm orderliness embodied in love and worship. Jesus came to restore that order of things for us on earth so that Creation could step aside from the noise that tears us apart and so praise the Lord our Creator for His marvellous deeds and be in tune with Him in the Dance. Praise the Lord in dance. "Let them praise his name with dancing", sang the Psalmist[1].

When I catalogued my brother's large number of photographs after his death I realised that here was a whole theme of Creation arising out of the silence of Heaven-the elements, the sky, the sea, mountains and hills, rivers and valleys, the seasons, "man's" response in worship and his activities, nature and animals each in their own way and all partaking in the Dance of the Universe. I knew then that I had to bring the whole theme to birth. Obviously it has to be selective according to the material at my disposal.

These passages are all personal reflections based on Christian teaching. They are not dogmatic or final but rather meant to lead each to his or her own reflections or meditations which can be used with or without the Biblical references and Questions to Think Through. Biblical references are from the New International Version unless otherwise stated.

My heartfelt thanks to Archbishop Rowan Williams for writing the Foreword when he is so busy and to all those who have been or are my spiritual mentors, to the late Bishop Edmund Morgan, Archbishop George Appleton and Canon Donald Allchin; also to the Rev'd Robert Green and Canon Stephen Sidebotham. I am also hugely indebted to my parents and my brother, Jim, for his perception of Creation, to Agata Salawa-Adam and her son Robert for hours of typing and the encouragement given to me, to Graham Osborn who has kindly helped with sundry matters, to those who have submitted their photographs and to Angela Legood for proof reading, and many friends who have also encouraged me on my spiritual journey.

[1] Psalm 149 v 3

PROLOGUE

"THE LORD OF THE DANCE"

I danced in the morning when the world was begun,
and I danced in the moon and the stars and the sun,
and I came down from heaven and I danced on earth :
at Bethlehem I had my birth.

> *"Dance, then, wherever you may be,*
> *I am the Lord of the Dance" said He,*
> *"and I'll lead you all, wherever you may be,*
> *and I'll lead you all in the dance" said He.*

From "The Lord of the Dance" – Sydney Carter

"The Dance of Life"
Mlini, near Dubrovnik, Croatia

I CREATION

A THE DANCE BEGINS

1.THE BIRTH OF THE UNIVERSE

Early morning scene, Maidstone, Kent

LORD, that moment when Your Spirit was brooding over the face of the Universe and You said "Let there be light "[1] was the birth of our Creation. Just as at the birth of a child there was that same sheer delight as You exhilarated over Your handiwork, shot through as it was with light and glory. You saw at each turn that what You had created was good – the separation of light and darkness;earth, sea and sky;vegetation; sun, moon and stars;creatures in the sea and on the land;then Your crowning achievement of human beings in Your own image[2,] for You breathed Your Spirit – Your very Life into us. And so the Dance of Life began.

When I ponder such mighty acts I am overwhelmed by the privilege and responsibility that You have bestowed upon us as stewards of Your workmanship[3].

As I look at the world today I see that it requires a life-time of repentance and sorrow for what we have done to despoil it and still do. Yet our one hope lies in another Birth – that of Your Son some 2, 000 years ago. Through His sacrificial Death we have the joy of Salvation – of being saved from this awful debt – starting here and now yet awaiting the final dawning of Your New Era when men and women from "east and west and north and south"[4] will sit at Your Heavenly Wedding[5].

[1] Genesis 1 v 3
[2] see Genesis 1 v 26
[3] see Genesis 2 v 15
[4] Luke 13 v 29
[5] see ibid and Revelation 19 vv 7 & 9

2. "LET THERE BE LIGHT"

Dawn over Kent

Sunrise over the Weald, Kent

WHEN I look at such an explosion of light and colour in the sky I marvel and see it as Your handiwork, Lord. The contrast between light and dark brings to mind the time when You separated them. "Let there be light"[1] You said and "there was light"[1] – Your Light, Your Word and Your authority in Creation. And they still have that same power. Your Heavens, Your very Creation still declare Your majesty and Your Reign. There, amid so great a display we can see resplendent light. Yes, and Your Son declared "I am the light of the world"[2] Who lightens and enlightens each one of us[1].

Yet, as I peer further into such a sky, I wonder how it is that we, created as we are by You, could be so blind to Your glory and Your Lordship as to disobey Your every command..." Let there be light", let there be purity, a response of love to Your Love for creating us in such an amazing, awe-inspiring world where sun, moon and stars are telling of Your splendour[3] and dancing in harmony with Your tune.

So, Lord, I look to You to illumine me, to guide me and to be a beacon for me when the way ahead is not clear. And in turn I know that You ask of me that I should be a shining lantern to those who live in the dark, awaiting the dawning of Your Eternal Light in their lives (even if they do not realise it) so that they, too, may carry on the Dance which You, its Lord, began.

[1] Genesis 1 v 3 and see John 1 vv 1-5, 9
[2] John 9 v 5
[3] see Psalm 19 and Haydn's "Creation"

3. THE ARTISTRY OF CREATION

LORD, Your many faceted works fill me with awe and wonder. Every day I see and learn something new. Just as in this delicate interweaving of branches and leaves, so is Your Creation. Each little section shows some different nuance and aspect of the world about me and the more I look the more I realise the amazing diversity and intricacy of Your craftsmanship, demonstrating that such grandeur could not be the work of mere humans nor of chance. The sheer artistry of it all fills me with ecstasy when I gaze into each vignette of Nature as it plays out the Dance of Life.

No leaf, no twig, branch or tree is the same and like this tree we too are "fearfully and wonderfully made"[1] . Being unique each and every organism makes its own contribution to Your world – a veritable tapestry woven and interwoven across the pages of history, adding to or, all too often sadly, taking away from the glories of Your Universe.

Heavenly Father, help me by the power of Your Holy Spirit to make a worthy input to Your Kingdom Life and so spread its values amongst those with whom I come into contact.

[1] Psalm 139 v 14

4. THE ELEMENTS PERFORMING THE WORD OF THE LORD

SUCH a mystic glow and interplay of cloud only serves to demonstrate Your finger, Lord, in shaping the world. Each ripple of cloud is as the shimmer of Your Spirit hovering over Your Creation[1] and then moving out across the earth revealing Your secrets to those who have eyes and ears attuned[2]. And like those ever-rolling clouds so is Your ever-roving

Spirit, reminding us that we are a pilgrim people with no abiding place in this life[3]. Just as Your eagle eye is watching over us[4], shedding Your rays into our minds, so You give us Your Word to warn, advise, encourage and gladden us to go and move on, taking Your Word of justice and love to those who know You not.

The subtlety of light, colour and tone in each cloud declares Your omnipresence. However, sometimes these clouds are darkness overshadowing the sun. Then the way ahead appears dim and, as in the foregathering of those storm clouds over land and sea, so we ponder the mystery of the forces of nature which lie beyond our control such as floods, earthquake, wind, fire and tidal changes. Even so You have given us the intellect to gain the knowledge and skills which enable us to predict and plan ahead against most of these powerful elements. At other times the sun pierces the clouds with radiant light and Your glory is once again revealed, pointing us ever onwards. Nevertheless whether the darkness hides You or the light reveals more of You and beckons us on, we know that beyond this veil lies the full radiance of Your Divinity waiting for us to be ready to receive that deeper illumination.

Then too, we can take up the Dance of Life with all the agents of Your Creation which perform Your Word – sunshine and showers, wind and snow, hail and ice, thunder and lightning. All these give us different glimpses of Your fashioning, teaching us something more about You and Your Universe for we see

"Thy justice like mountains high soaring above
Thy clouds which are fountains of goodness and love "[5]

[1] see Genesis 1 vv 1 & 2
[2] see John 1 vv 9-14
[3] see Hebrews 11 v 13 : 1 Peter 2 v 11
[4] see Jeremiah 1 v 12
[5] From "Immortal, Invisible, God only Wise"

B LIVING CREATION LIFE

1. FROM INFANCY TO THE HEAT OF THE DAY
-TRANSGRESSION

Farming well done

Desolation

Desecration

HEAVENLY FATHER, so often we think we know best. And when I look at the neat furrows of a ploughed field or a piece of work well done, it would seem that we are indeed working in harmony with You and Nature. Yes, and we can be pleased with such an achievement if we have done it in accordance with Your will and we give You all the honour for aiding us. It is certainly satisfying and rewarding, and hopefully through it Your Kingdom can grow.

Yet we also know what a mess we can make of things. Our own and vested interests get in the way-selfishness, greed, envy, jealousy, anger-and soon the world about us is in a tangled state. Sometimes we can see the light behind the contortion and we turn back to You. At other times there is just a barren fog of dissatisfaction, malaise, warfare – and the fields of envy, hatred, bitterness and killing continue to grow.

So Lord, I would pray that You will keep us from temptation and from the evil within and without and guide us along the straight and narrow way. Send Your Holy Spirit to help us in all our doings and fill us with Your holy and loving wisdom as we seek to do Your will and declare Your Good News to all peoples, so that swords may be turned into ploughshares[1] and the harmony of the Universe be restored in each of us so that the Dance may continue and the whole world be in tune with Yourself.

[1] see Micah 4 v 3b

2.   THE CROSS AND FORGIVENESS

ABBA FATHER, it passes beyond all comprehension to come to terms with the fact that You undertook to die such a cruel death on a Cross to save us from spiritual annihilation. There are some things that one simply cannot understand but just looking up at Your Cross speaks right into our hearts. How can we fail to be moved to see such Love hanging there so poignantly and at the same time so generously saying Abba, "Father, forgive them, for they do not know what they are doing"[1].

As I peer into this scene depicting the Crucifixion with Your Son hanging between two renegades I see yet another Cross and I realise that that one stands there for myself. I too have had my share in crucifying Him, Who is my Saviour, and I must needs undergo a crucifixion of myself to become more like Him. Only thus can I - and each one of us - return love for Love, be forgiven and enter into Your Kingdom. Thus pardoned, cleansed and restored can we show forth Your radiance and Your Love to a cruel and hurting world...

Forgive me, dear Lord, for my part in bringing about Your Son's crucifixion and thank You for Your loving generosity towards me and all mankind.

[1] Luke 23 v 34

3. RESURRECTION AND TRANSFIGURATION

Sunset and Dawn over Kentish scenery

HEAVENLY FATHER, as the crimson rays of the setting sun sank over Your Son's dying Body, foreclosing His life on earth, so it was that soon the golden rays of dawn heralded His rising from the dead. Since death could not hold Him down at this dawning of a new age there was a mighty rending of the spicèd tomb where He had been placed and in an instant the sun rose more sharply over against where He had lain and the Dance continued.

Yes, indeed, a new era had broken forth as He indicated to Mary Magdalene in the Garden. "Do not hold on to me"[1], He said. Don't cling onto Me – to the earthly Jesus you knew for I am awaiting the time when I return to "My Father and your Father, to my God and your God"[2] to establish My Reign of Love...When I am ascended back to My Father you will receive the Spirit and you will be transformed into powerful witnesses for Me[3]...

I see dear Lord, that it is our task to continue that work as we look forward to the time when the world will be transfigured and changed from glory to glory – humankind, all living creatures and even Nature itself[4]. So the serpent will lose its sting and men and women will live in harmony with all Creation and reign with You in Your Eternal Kingdom[5].

HALLELUIAH !

[1] John 20 v 17
[2] John 20 v 17
[3] see Acts 1 v 8
[4] see Romans 8 vv 22& 23
[5] see Isaiah 11 vv 1-10

II NATURE

1. THE SKY

From Dawn Till Dusk

English cloud effects in Kent

English cloud effects in Kent

Storm clouds over Dungeness, Kent

Sunset in Norway

Kentish sunset

"AND God said, 'Let there be an expanse between the waters to separate water from water'... and He 'called the expanse the "sky"'[1] ...When I behold all the different aspects of sky from a glorious clear azure blue to every kind of cloud formation, sunrise and sunset, it fills me with a sense of mystery. I stand awe-inspired at the range, from a sense of beauty and infinity on seeing the ethereal nature of such skies to a sense of frailty and the puny estate of mankind. When there are no clouds I peer in wonder at the sun, moon and stars. When dark storm clouds roll on towards me it makes me realise just how dependent we are on You, Lord. So, too, the Psalmist appreciated Your nearness or feared Your wrath with storm cloud, wind and rain performing Your

Word[2]. Yes, all the elements of the Universe are subject to the laws of Nature, each with its own part to play even if I am not always able to understand some of the more vehement forces like hurricanes or tornadoes as they hurtle across the sky in a world which the Bible tells us shares in the "fall" of mankind[3] . Yet You have endowed us with the ability to learn about the elements and act with wisdom where possible.

Sky and clouds played their part in Your Son's life too, just as they had done over the centuries before He came[4]. Angels appeared in the sky at His Birth[5], and a certain star led the Wise Men to Him[6]. You spoke out of the cloud at His Baptism[7] and when He was transfigured[8]. The sky turned dark with thunder clouds at His Crucifixion[9]. He entered into a cloud and rose up into the heavens at His Ascension[10]. And He said that He would return on the clouds in the sky[1]. He showed too, that we knew how to interpret the weather but not the signs of the time[12]...How important then is the role of the sky in revealing Your presence, even though unseen.

So dear Lord, please help me to appreciate not just the beauty and infinite variety of the sky and clouds but also that You inhabit them as indeed every part of Your Creation and have used the elements as signs of Your involvement in Your Son's life and are ultimately in control of the forces of Nature. I perceive the vastness of infinity and that though You are hidden from us by the splendour and intensity of light, I give You thanks for manifesting Your presence to us through Your Son's life.

[1] Genesis 1 vv 6-8
[2] see Psalm 148 v 8
[3] see Romans 8 vv 18-22
[4] see Exodus 14 vv 19 & 20: 19 v 16 : 2 Kings 2 v 11
[5] see Luke 2 vv 8-15
[6] see Matthew 2 vv 1-12
[7] see Matthew 3 vv 16&17 et al
[8] see Matthew 17 vv 1-8 et al
[9] see Matthew 27 vv 51-53 et al: see also John 12 vv 28-29
[10] see Acts 1 v 9
[11] see Matthew 26 v 64 et al
[12] see Luke 12 vv 54-56

2.   THE SEA

A wild sea at Dungeness, Kent

Peaceful   sea   in   Norway

"O LORD, how manifold are thy works! in wisdom hast thou made them all: the earth is full of thy riches. So is this great and wide sea, wherein are things creeping innumerable, both small and great beasts"[1] ...A whole world and ecosystem exists on and in the depths of the oceans, as for example, along the Barrier Reefs around the world with their subterranean passages and lanes. They all serve to manifest the enormity of Your Creation, Lord, and make me want to exclaim, "What is man, that thou art mindful of him?"[2].

The sea seems to be dominated by the same situations as on dry land. It is subject to the sun and moon's laws of ebb and flow just as gravity controls the whole of the earth. There are storms and tempests as well as a serenity which surpasses our aspirations. And there are tensions, strife and killings by the creatures in it much as on earth. Yet I know that You are in control, as Your Son showed when He calmed a severe storm on the Sea of Galilee[3] and when He walked on the same sea amid a squall but as soon as He entered the disciples' boat the waves and wind subsided[4].

So, Lord, You have shown me that when I invite You to be involved in my life, whatever is happening, the storms and hurts in and around me can be calmed and dealt with. Please help me to remember this and to welcome You into my "boat" constantly so that I can relax knowing that You are at the controls and I can be in tune with the Dance of Life, of which You are the Architect and Choreographer.

[1] Psalm 104 vv 24&25 Authorised Version
[2] Psalm 8 v 4 Authorised Version
[3] see Mark 4 vv 35-41 et al
[4] see Mark 6 vv 45-53 et al

3. THE COAST

Norwegian coast line

Norwegian coastal sunset

Skomer -off the coast in South Wales

I NEVER cease to be amazed, Lord, at the variety and beauty of our coastline here in the British Isles and round the world. It is good that some of it is flat with stretches of shingle or sandy beaches where one can relax and breathe in Your Divine air. Yet, it is also the sheer ruggedness of so much of it that causes my spirit to soar in wonderment at such grandeur, such varied design, shape and colour. Once again it makes me realise the immensity of Your creative activity and I want to reach out to You in Your infinity and glorious splendour. As I look out over these scenes, watch the effect of wind, sea and waves along the coastline as they fulfil Your Word, I can drink in the regal vistas and be mesmerised by the huge colonies of sea birds there may be. Then too, I can begin to enter into the silence of Eternity as I perceive these alluring views.

In the presence of such majestic sights I feel exhilarated and caught up in a timeless world, despite the rigours of life along our shorelines. They take me beyond myself and into Your incomparable transcendence and otherness.

Heavenly Father, help me to keep my eyes fixed on You, to bow before Your Sovereignty and to live within the boundaries of Your innately pertinent Laws, just as the coast line sets limits between land and sea.

4. MOUNTAINS AND HILLS

Mountain scenes near Bilbao, Spain

Hills in the Lake District

"I WILL lift up mine eyes unto the hills, from whence cometh my help. My help cometh from the Lord, which made heaven and earth"[1]. So sang the Psalmist and so too, the people of the Old Testament. They knew, Lord, that Your servants Moses[2] and Elijah[3] had had mountain top experiences and encountered You there. Such occasions would serve to make it easier for Your Son's disciples to accept that He would be with them or appear to them on a mountain top, even if the encounter was tinged with fear. (It appears that in Old Testament times you would die if you were to see Yourself or any of Your agents, for example, angels.) Peter had already declared that Your Son was the Messiah, "the Son of the living God "[4], hence they might well feel afraid when He was transfigured before them, shining brightly like the sun [5]. And later He led His disciples out to a mountain and whilst talking with them was lifted up and He ascended back to Heaven[6].

So mountains and hills conjure up for me Your Presence, Your Divinity and Power, Your might and majesty. As I look at distant peaks I feel an energy and strength reaching out to me and suggesting that I reach the mountain top to explore my vocation. It is indeed, as I gaze, that I can have flights of fancy or, more importantly, if I am tuned in to You, I can start to comprehend how a dream can be turned into reality, begin to understand how and what You might be leading me to be or do, or just to drink in Your Presence and so be changed.

I long to acknowledge that Presence all the time, Lord, but especially precious are the times when You reveal Yourself to me in a mountain top experience (whether physically there or metaphorically in another situation). Then I can peer beyond the fog that might be in my mind to the distant scene of our Heavenly home.

[1] Psalm 121 vv 1-2 Authorised Version
[2] see Exodus 19 vv 3-6
[3] see 1 Kings 19 vv 8-13
[4] Matthew 16 v 16
[5] see Mark 9 vv 2-13 et al
[6] see Matthew 28 vv 16-20

5.   VALLEYS AND PLAINS

A Valley in the Lake District

A Kentish Plain

SINCE so many of the human race live in valleys, plains or flat areas of the world rather than the mountain tops or plâteaux, I see that there have to be important reasons for this, such as the need for water and fish from the rivers and seas, hunting for food, farming and industry. And so smaller or larger communities grew up over the centuries.

I feel really blessed to be able to walk along the valleys and plains with perhaps views of mountains and hills, a river meandering through their midst and cornfields with ripening grain[1]. Yet all too often it seems that sadly many of those havens have become despoiled by industry. I know we need it but perhaps more thought could go into where and how an area might be developed? The prophet Isaiah had wonderful visions in which he saw that You, Lord, were at work re-creating the world and that the valleys and plains would share in the redemption of mankind[2] and barren, parched deserts would once again flourish. "The wilderness will rejoice and blossom...Water will gush forth in the wilderness...And a highway will be there; it will be called the Way of Holiness...only the redeemed will walk there"[3].

Lord, thank You for the valleys and plains where most of us live our lives. I see that they keep us on the straight and narrow way. A "mountain top" experience is indeed so wonderful yet we spend much of our time living normal lives and have to hold on to those instances of elation when going through the valleys or difficult occasions. Thank You that the unproductive and waste places in my life can be redeemed as I put my trust in You and align my will with Yours, so that I can move in tune with Your Dance.

[1] see Psalm 65 v 13
[2] see Isaiah 35
[3] Isaiah 35 vv 1b, 6b, 8, 9b

6. RIVERS

River running into the sea at Mlini near Dubrovnik, Croatia

River scene, Winchester,
Hampshire

Aysgarth Falls, Yorkshire
Margaret Doak

RIVERS conjure up for me so many different images and scenes such as catching fish, gliding along in or rowing a boat on one, walking alongside them with friends or on one's own. As David said "The Lord is my shepherd;I shall not want. He maketh me to lie down in green pastures: he leadeth me beside the still waters"[1] – Wonderful places to meditate on a sunny day. However, over the centuries, people who gathered together to form a community round a river have grown in numbers and larger towns and industry have grown up often ruining the countryside. Obviously these are necessary but sadly, as with valleys and plains many areas were developed without thought for the environment.

Above all I am learning though, dear Lord, how Your Son applied rivers to our spiritual lives. Already, I have seen that You are my Shepherd and that You care for all my wants and lead me by still waters. Yet so often the Israelites of old must have seen the rivers, like the Jordan, dried up and the land surrounding it parched. Nevertheless, Your Son gave us a new vision, that when our lives are dried up spiritually, He can supply us with living water for "Whoever believes in me, as the Scripture has said, streams of living water will flow from within him"[2].The Spirit would enhance and transform our lives, and enable our spirits to overflow with love, joy and peace. Water being so important for our lives both physically and spiritually is also viewed by the writer of Revelation to be an integral part in the consummation of Your Kingdom when "The river of the water of life, as clear as crystal" shall flow "from the throne of God and of the Lamb down the middle of the great street of the city"[3]. And because it makes everything so fertile the tree of life will bear crops of fruit every month and "the leaves of the tree are for the healing of the nations"[3].

Thank You Lord for providing us with the pleasures and uses of rivers. Grant that we may learn not to pollute them nor allow them to dry up by our over-use of them but to be good stewards of them for the sake of our environment and the service they provide us with. Furthermore I see how You, Your Son and the Holy Spirit can act like a river in my spiritual life and fill me to overflowing with all good gifts for my spirit. May I be truly thankful and may Your living water renew my spirit.

[1] Psalm 23 vv 1&2 Authorised Version
[2] John 7 vv 37&38
[3] Revelation 22 vv 1& 2

30

7. ISLANDS

Islands off the coast near Dubrovnik, Croatia

*Bardsey Island off the Llyn Peninsula;
Island of a thousand saints, North Wales
Margaret Doak*

LORD, I perceive that mankind has always been adventurous to find out what was beyond the horizon, whether on land or sea. So it was that both larger and smaller islands off the mainland or far out into the ocean came to be inhabited. Yet some of them may even have been settled with people before they were detached from the mainland. Whichever- there will always have been a certain struggle for existence, sometimes leading to battles. The smaller the island the more the inhabitants had to learn to be observant of times, seasons and weather conditions and to be reliant on a Power greater than themselves for their provisions. Many today are learning that that Power is You, Lord.

How much we still need to learn not to control Nature but to be aware of the elements performing their work so that we can find ways of avoiding or overcoming the more vehement aspects for those living in such places. Many islanders would never want to change a way of life lived in close proximity to Nature. Sadly, however, sometimes life has been so harsh that they have had little option but to leave, especially when basic materials could not reach them such as on the Island of St Kilda off the North Coast of Scotland nearly a century ago.

Heavenly Father, I have so much to glean from those who live this kind of life – resilience, wisdom, observance of times and seasons, knowledge of how to care for and feed oneself and the family – indeed how to live in harmony with Nature and one's fellow inhabitants. A holistic way of life if based on Your Laws. Not a few have gone off to smaller islands to live a life dedicated to You in communities or as hermits, drawn there for the silence and solitude they offer. In these situations they would hope to find their place in You and amid their praise make intercession for themselves, others and the world. I see their life of prayer as an entering into the Kingdom and believing it to be within them. Thank You, Lord, for the island spaces in my life wherein I can begin to relate more deeply to You.

III   THE FOUR SEASONS

A   WINTER

1. OUT OF SILENCE

Kentish sunrise
and
Kentish sunset

IN due time Your Almighty Word leapt out of silence[1] Lord. I see that Your Creation began with Your Word... "Let there be light"[2].So the Dance of life began. Then, at just the right time Your Word, Jesus, appeared on the scene on our planet Earth, "In the beginning was the

Word, and the Word was with God, and the Word was God"[3]. His disciples declared that Jesus, "The Word was made flesh, and dwelt among us, (and we behold his glory, the glory as of the only begotten of the Father,) full of grace and truth"[4]. They not only saw His glory but they handled Him, touched Him and heard Him speak[5] as Your Word, for He said "I am the Light of the World"[6]; "the Way and the Truth and the Life"[7]...

I know that it took centuries of preparation for You to send Your Son for that short space of some thirty years on earth and then a mere two to three years of Ministry. I marvel at what He achieved in that time – indeed, the redemption of the world from the claws of the devil. Yet I see too, that in the first place You had a plan – "The Lamb that was slain from the creation of the world"[8] was to work our Salvation. And during all that time You were progressively inspiring the Jewish leaders and prophets with Your Divine understanding. Then Jesus came and through His close relationship with You whilst on earth and His obedience, even unto death, wrought that Salvation by His Life, Death, Resurrection and Ascension.

Dear Father, through this insight I realise more than ever just how important are the times of preparation (sometimes over years), of immersing ourselves in Your Presence, Your Word and Your Love. Then there is the need to ascertain Your Will and plans for the advancement of Your Kingdom and our small part in this...Like the seeds which we know can only bear fruit by being allowed to await the appropriate time to germinate in silence in the ground, so I perceive You watching over Your Word for it to be fulfilled[9]. Then at the right moment after what may seem to be of endless waiting – even barrenness as in a long winter, there will be a sudden bursting forth into a panoply of ecstatic beauty and viridity both in the physical and the spirit-filled life.

[1] see Wisdom 18 v 15 (Apocrypha)
[2] Genesis 1 v 3 and see Chapter I A 1 & 2
[3] John 1 v 1
[4] John 1 v 14 Authorised Version
[5] see I John 1 v 1
[6] John 9 v 5
[7] John 14 v 6
[8] Revelation 13 v 8
[9] see Jeremiah 1 v 12

34

2. "IN THE BLEAK MID-WINTER" [1] - BIRTH

"While Shepherds Watched their Flocks by Night....Glory shone around "

Nativity scene, Prague
Margaret Doak

IT began with a BIRTH. Tradition has it that You were born in the winter, Jesus, and the timing seems to fit well, being placed at the end of the winter solstice and the Jewish festival of Light to celebrate it. So I can accept that You, Who are the Light of the World, may have come in the dead of winter, just at the point when light begins to creep back into the sky. And You bring the hope of new life to the seared and parched earth and to our spirits, tainted as they are with sin and wrong-doing.

With Your Birth lies the promise then of a new beginning. Angels announced it, shepherds tending their sheep by night– "In the bleak mid-winter"– as we sing[1], heard the message, saw and believed Who You were. So too, Wise Men, guided by a star[2].They were all so thrilled and encouraged. Were their lives changed, did they pass on the Good News, did they remember Your Birth;were the younger shepherds amongst Your disciples when You started preaching? Were seeds sown where the Wise Men came from or did they all just sink into oblivion?

Sadly so many of us hear the Good News with joy but never allow it to make a difference in our lives. Forgive us, dear Lord, for our callousness and grant that seeds sown may indeed bear fruit so that Your Light may shine in the world through our witness.

[1] From the carol "In the Bleak Mid-Winter": see Luke 2 vv 1-20
[2] see Matthew 2 vv 1-12

B SPRING

1. "LIKE WHEAT THAT SPRINGETH GREEN"[1]

Green wheat growing in Kent
Margaret Doak

JUST as the farmers of old, You, Lord Jesus, sow seed in a variety of situations and it is received in different ways. Your Divine spark exists in each one of us and again, like the farmers of old and today You know that there is a still point – a waiting time in which Your Word can penetrate, germinate, grow and flower. Sometimes it will spring up and mature quickly, sometimes more slowly. Yet, whichever, if there is endurance and persistence, a good crop, or character – will mature in due season[2].

So You ask of us, like a sportsman training daily, patience, perseverance and endurance, often amid set backs, tests, trials, maybe persecutions. Those who hold on steadfastly find an enrichment beyond all imaginings. We thank You for those who have done so and have received the crown of life.

Help us dear Lord to persevere, with Your grace, when the going is hard and to rejoice at all times, believing that all things work together to produce a wonderful crop and so continue the Dance which builds up Your Kingdom.

[1] From "Now the Green Blade Riseth from the Buried Grain"
[2] see Mark 4 vv 1-20 et al

2. EASTER – "THE QUEEN OF SEASONS, BRIGHT"[1]

Garden Tomb in Jerusalem
Margaret Doak

"Then went in also that other disciple … and he saw, and believed"[1]

I am exhilarated and captivated year after year by the mystery of Nature renewing herself afresh from that period of resting during the winter. And never more so than after a severe winter of cold winds, snow and ice. Whilst I see these as indeed agents of Your Creation, dear Lord, performing Your Word, as the Psalmist says[1], and as an essential part of Your climate plan, yet they also expose our fragility and the necessity for us to be ever mindful of our dependence on You for all aspects of our lives. Nevertheless, anticipation turns our expectations and waiting into joy in Nature at the first signs of new life – the first lambs, the first blade of corn, the first snowdrops and crocuses. Warm rain and sun too, herald the rise to fresh beginnings with all the colours that flowers and blossoms can muster.

Yet, there is also a darker side to Spring. Young lambs in particular at this time of the year in the prime of their lives are separated off to become meat for us. Sometimes I can hardly bear the thought of those little woolly bodies leaping and prancing in tune with the Dance of Life being cut off in their prime – like the lambs for sacrifice in former days.

How much more then, Jesus, Your Son, Who was sacrificed for us to redeem us, set us free from sin and sickness and restore us to a right relationship with You, our Heavenly Father. Yet surely we are so blessed to live in the light of that awesome rending of the tomb heralding the Resurrection. And so You set a seal on the chasm of past darkness separating us-humankind-from You. Your dear Son's Resurrection gives us the TRUE joy in the True Spring-

"'T is the Spring of souls today;
Christ hath burst his prison,
And from three days' sleep in death
As a Sun hath arisen."[2]

[1] See Psalm 147 v15
[2] John 20 v 8 Authorised Version
[3] "Come ye Faithful, Raise the Strain"

C SUMMER

1. HALCYON DAYS

LORD, every year I look forward to those long summer days when we can relax a little and enjoy being out in Your beautiful creation. The crops have been planted and there is a space of time before they are harvested. Many of us, including farmers, still work, though others wind down for a few weeks over the school holidays and try to draw breath.

Yet, should we be so relaxed that we forget that summer is also the time when we should take stock of our spiritual fruit? Some 700-800 years before Your Son appeared on earth, Amos, when You asked him what he saw, replied "A basket of ripe fruit"[1]. Is not this a season then, when we should be ensuring that our spiritual lives are bearing fruit before the great and final harvest?You had a great deal to say to Amos about the state of affairs amongst the rich in the Israel of his day and I hear You saying much the same to us, especially here in the West where many of us still have so much even amid times of economic uncertainty and yet where we all too often grumble about things.

Father, I know that I need to look to myself to see if the fruit of the Spirit is ripening in my own life – fruit of "love, joy, peace, patience, kindness, goodness, faithfulness, gentleness and self-control"[2]. I once read a caption which said that You want "spiritual fruits not religious nuts"[3] which I see are hard to crack. Please help me, dear Lord, to produce loving, gentle but firm fruit for the sake of Your Kingdom.

[1] Amos 8 v 2
[2] Galatians 5 vv 22-23
[3] Found on a bookmark-caption by Ethel Wilcox (source untraceable)

2. THE FIRST FRUITS OF HARVEST

FESTIVALS played an important part in Your Son's life on earth, Lord. The overall impression is one of joy and thanksgiving on those occasions when the whole community would gather together and sing appropriate psalms, such as "You call forth songs of joy"[1] and at harvest festivals, "You care for the land and water it; you enrich it abundantly. The streams of God are filled with water to provide the people with corn, for so you have ordained it. You drench its furrows and level its ridges:you soften it with showers and bless its crops. You crown the year with your bounty and your carts overflow with abundance"[2]. Praise indeed, for often there were droughts in Israel.

We see just how vital it was then, as it still is today, to offer thanks to You for providing the sun and the rain for the crops and fruits to grow and for animals and fish to grow and reproduce.

Lord, we toil and work hard to produce our food and despite any set backs caused by the weather, we have every reason to be thankful. Too often we take our harvest here in the West for granted as also the arrival of food and drink on the shelves of our supermarkets and grocers and grumble at the prices. However, do we not need to look again and see at what cost some of it has reached us-often from the Third World where there are frequent droughts, floods or other disasters, just as there were in Biblical times and which I see are all part of the course of Nature? Sadly, all too often the workers are rewarded with a pittance. Yes, life is so unfair, yet need it be so? I believe that You have provided enough resources for all the world if only we would learn how to share it out fairly and act before it is too late.

[1] Psalm 65 v 8
[2] Psalm 65 vv 9-11

D   AUTUMN

1. "SEASON OF MISTS AND MELLOW FRUITFULNESS" [1]

Autumn near Maidstone, Kent

AUTUMN-yes

"Season of mists and mellow fruitfulness!
Close bosom-friend of the maturing sun;...
Where are the songs of Spring?Ay, where are they?
Think not of them, thou hast thy music too"[1].

Indeed, Autumn has its own sweet music and can produce warm, glowing sunny days with golden colours on the trees. It is the time when I see that people begin to work in earnest again. Summer holidays are over and for many it is the season of new beginnings – at school, at university, at work, in Parliament, even perhaps in our spiritual lives. Fresh hope, yet I see it also as the in-gathering of the harvest: corn for our "daily bread" of which dear Jesus, You said, "This is my body given for you; do this in remembrance of me"[2] : and the grapes for the wine of which You said "This is my blood of the (new) covenant which is poured out for many for the forgiveness of sins"[3].

I know, Lord Jesus, how much I need to give thanks to You for Your sacrificial Death to procure our Salvation from sin and sickness and for the harvest which produces that bread and wine. May Your Holy Spirit inspire us to be truly grateful.

[1] "Ode to Autumn" by John Keats (Everyman's Library 1944 edition)
[2] Luke 22 v 19
[3] Matthew 26 vv 27b-28

2. THE FINAL REAPING

DEAR Lord, Your Son told several parables about harvest and the final reaping and He said that although farmers sow good seed yet often there appear weeds in the midst of the growing crops. These weeds, He stressed, should be allowed to grow till the harvest lest in rooting them out some of the wheat might also be rooted out. So too, with a catch of fish-some good and some bad. He warned us that at the end of the Age there would be a final separation, good wheat into barns and weeds collected into bundles for burning[1]. Likewise, good fish into baskets and bad fish to be thrown into the fiery furnace where there will be weeping and gnashing of teeth[1]. The choice, I hear You say, is ours.

Yes, Lord, I know that You are a God of Love. You love the world so much that You gave Your Son, not to condemn it but to save it through Him. To whoever believes in Him, You promised Eternal Life[2]. Yet I also hear You saying that not to believe in Jesus if one has come to know Him is to bring condemnation on oneself[2]. I see this as meaning a deliberate turning away from Him, not living life in accordance with the way of Life that He has shown us.

When I ponder on Your dear Son's sacrifice, I think, how could one reject such Love? Alas, all too often and easily we give in to our free will. Temptation can appear so pleasant and life has taught many of us hard and unloving lessons so we fall short of Your Love. Please help me, through Your Spirit, to live a life of that same unselfish Love as Jesus and gratitude to Him, which will shine through to others and reflect Your Glory as they see us involved in the Dance which is Eternity.

[1] see Matthew 13 vv 24-30 ; 36-43 ; 47-50
[2] see John 3 vv 16-18

IV   PRAYER AND WORSHIP

1.   WORSHIP IN NATURE

Mountain scene – Norway

Waves crashing against rocks. Near Dubrovnik, Croatia

Sheffield Park, Sussex

WHEN I am out and about in Your Creation, Lord, I understand why people have worshipped and prayed to You from time immemorial, either out of awe for the grandeur surrounding them or through fear of the elements. One can feel deep harmony with Nature on one occasion but be afraid of the storms another day. So, early "man" must have prayed accordingly and so too Your people, the Israelites of old. They saw on the one hand "the mountains and hills will burst into song before you, and all the trees of the field will clap their hands"[1]. On the other hand the Psalmist saw that "The seas have lifted up, O Lord, the seas have lifted up their voice;the seas have lifted up their pounding waves". Yet the same psalm recognises "Mightier than the thunder of the great waters, mightier than the breakers of the sea - the Lord on high is mighty"[2].

So Your Son's Disciples found in a sharp storm on the Sea of Galilee. Their terror at the suddenness and violence of that storm led them to cry out to Him and at once He stilled it. I pray that we might find it within us to have the faith that the Disciples lacked at that moment (but found later), so that You will still the storms of our lives today...

As I sit and ponder on a hill top, view a rugged mountain scene, relax under a tree like Abraham, who believed that You would communicate with him there, or by the sea, whether it is calm or the waves are crashing on the rocks, I look into the vastness of Your Eternity. Time seems to stretch out into infinity and the magnitude and majesty of it fills me with reverence and wonder at Your hand which fashioned our Universe, and I am impelled to worship You in silent adoration. I cannot find words but I feel transfixed, even transported by the beauty, the shapes and awesome artistry of it all. It takes me into a totally other dimension for I am at once as small as a pebble on the beach and yet at the same time very special to You, for You have created me, and each one of us, to be unique and precious to You. Thank You Lord, as the Dance goes on.

[1] Isaiah 55 v 12b
[2] Psalm 93 vv 3 & 4

2.   CHURCH AND CONGREGATION

Part of Congregational Carol Service, Margaret Doak

"Where two or three are gathered in My name" [1]
St Beunos Church, Clynnog Fawr Llyn Peninsula, North Wales,
Margaret Doak

Holy Cross Church, Bearsted
Doug Chenery

THE scene shifts. I know that I can meet with You, Lord in the beauty of Creation – or indeed anywhere. Yet, I also feel the need for a place where worship has been and is being offered to give me that sense of otherness, of holiness, of serenity and awe – a place where I can soak up Your Presence, learn more about You in the stillness and find out perhaps what Your will is for me.

Nevertheless, that is only one side of a relationship with You, for You said "Where two or three are gathered together in my name, there am I in the midst of them"[1] as Lord of the cosmic Dance with Your dancers. So I see the fellowship I have with other believers is of paramount importance to me if I and they are to find You today. And praise and worship, I can see, not only give You the glory but also build up Your Church wherever it meets to worship. It also helps and encourages me in my daily walk with You and builds up my discipleship, knowing that others have the same joys and problems and share in the way forward, as well as supporting me in my belief and understanding of You and Your will. Perhaps we have at times encapsulated You in the beauty of the architecture of churches but they also inspire me to realise that You are indeed with us individually and with the body of worshippers.

So dear Lord, please give me the desire to find You within me and at the same time in communion with Your other friends and in a mystical union with others around the world.

[1] Matthew 18 v 20 Authorised Version

3. THE BREAKING OF BREAD – THE EUCHARIST

Preparing for the Eucharist , Pistyll ,Llyn Peninsula,North Wales
Margaret Doak

PERHAPS the most important words You spoke, dear Jesus, were those uttered at the Last Supper You partook of with Your disciples-"Take and eat;this is my body....This is my blood of the (new) covenant, which is poured out for many for the forgiveness of sins"[1]. These words fill me with awe and wonder and indeed I see being present at Your special service as the pivotal point of my week. I know that You are with me all the time, yet here in the Eucharist You are both the Priest offering the Sacrifice and the Victim-the Sacrifice itself being offered to the Father on behalf of all of us. As we partake of Your very Being in a timeless union we can lay aside our earthly anxieties and worries, sins and failures and feel nurtured, washed and cleansed by You. I see it also as a spiritual union with all who make up Your Body, the Church, throughout the world and a place where all earth's sorrows can be caught up in Your sorrows and transformed. Indeed "There is joy for all the members In the sorrows of the Head"[2].

So I can understand that the whole act transcends our normal earthly life and we can begin to enter into that great silence where all is light and purity and out of which You came into the world[3]. It is an innovative, creative action where Heaven and Earth meet in a vibrant way and in which we are all caught up in the worship wherein the angels also share with us and all believers everywhere.

Lord Jesus, I know that however much I long to receive You into my very being, I can never be as prepared as I should be for such an awesome moment. Please help me to live my life day by day in close relationship with You so that I do not miss out on all that You have to offer me as I make contact with You in that mystical union which changes my life. Only thus can I become ever more like You as a sweet smelling fragrance,[4] dance in tune with You and so help to spread Your Kingdom.[5]

[1] Matthew 26 vv 26 b --- 28
[2] From "There's a Wideness in God's Mercy"
[3] see Wisdom 18 vv 14 & 15
[4] see Ephesians 5v 2
[5] see Anthony Duncan (Helios 1972) page 79 for this chapter

4. AIDS TO WORSHIP

Icon of the Trinity 13th Century
by Andrei Rublev of Russia

LORD, I am so blessed for even if I am unable to see You I have a whole plethora of aids that come to my rescue to help me in my daily encounter with You. First and foremost there is Your Holy Spirit. If I allow Him, He can give me that daily infilling to renew and revivify me. Only thus can I keep my relationship fanned into life, into love, joy, peace, patience[1] and welling up, bubbling up into the streams of living water that You promised[2]. What an awesome pledge.

However, just as in any human relationship I am also grateful for tangible and visible aids which can help to enhance my prayer life – such as Your Word in the Bible, the Church's worship, a crucifix, prayer books, hymns and choruses, pictures and paintings. All of these can spur me on. And then there are those paintings by men and women throughout the ages who, after hours of prayer and meditation under the influence of the Spirit, have produced icons, or images of Your Godhead as in this icon by Rublev, of Your Son's Life, Death, Resurrection and Ascension, of the coming of the Holy Spirit and of Your saints. Whether they are displayed on an iconostasis or icon-screen, or separately, they fill me with awe and wonder and I see myself as one of that vast number of members of Your Church praying around the clock and around the world. Either way they encourage me in my prayer and worship and my walk with You.

Dear Lord, my greatest desire is to offer You all the glory, to praise and thank You for what You have done for me and for the world. Help me to use all of these means at my disposal so that I can reflect Your glory to all about me and so carry on the Dance which is Your Kingdom.

[1] see Galatians 5 v 22
[2] see John 7 vv 38-39

5.   HOLY PLACES

*Church of the Holy Sepulchre,
Jerusalem*

*Shrine of St Melangell,
Pennant Melangell, Wales*

*Pilgrims at Llanengan, Llyn Peninsula,
North Wales*

*Healing Well also at Llanengan
All photographs by Margaret Doak*

LORD, I have been so privileged to have trodden where Your Son and saints have walked and I can only acknowledge such places as holy, even awesome. What makes them so I ask?. I perceive that when one approaches these sites, hallowed over the centuries, one is compelled to put aside all outward trappings and enter into an inner silence which links one with Your Divinity and Your Holiness. Prayer is indeed where we enter into a conscious relationship with You, dear Lord, and where we can transcend the ordinariness of our lives, whether with or without speech. Yet when we pray where prayer has been offered throughout the ages we may well enter into the depth of communication beyond our consciousness and entwined with those who have gone before us, so building up an atmosphere of a life beyond this world, nevertheless very much part of it. Indeed we find Lord, that You are both transcendent and immanent, holy and lofty, worthy of our praise and at the same time deeply involved in the affairs of our daily lives.

Silence indeed so often seems the only way that I can interact with You, learn and understand more of You and relate to You as Lord of the Universe of which I am a part. In this silence, which is Eternity, I need to "Let sense be dumb, let flesh retire"[1] so that You may ever "Speak through the earthquake, wind and fire, O still, small voice of calm"[1].

Be with me, Lord, in such places, for I perceive that where Your Son and saints have penetrated this silence then this has brought about holy deeds and miracles and so this space between Heaven and Earth has become a "thin space" – where both meet and the Dance continues.

[1] From "Dear Lord and Father of Mankind"

6. MONASTICISM

Holy Cross Church
Winchester, Hampshire
Once a monastic church

Looking towards the Sea of Galilee from
The Mount of Beatitudes. An area of calm
and solitude where Jesus might well have
prayed

Monastery in Spain

Margaret Doak

"ALL my fresh springs shall be in thee"[1]. So sang the Psalmist. Lord, I see that in space and silence Your Son surrounded His Life. He found His "fresh springs" in You by long hours of prayer[2], of communion with You in that inner depth of silence and solitude before a heavy day's work[2] and in His vocation as Suffering Servant[3]. That calling was to bring about the redemption and salvation of the world, of power-craving people and of those in abject poverty, both physically and spiritually. Indeed, He said "The Spirit of the Lord is upon me, because He hath anointed me to preach the Gospel to the poor; He hath sent me to heal the brokenhearted, to preach deliverance to the captives, and recovering of sight to the blind, to set at liberty them that are bruised"[4]. And often He would go off with His Disciples for a break, which would undoubtedly have included a time of prayer and teaching about it[5].

I understand that those who feel called to the monastic way of life believe that by entering into a community which is ordered by prayer, work and recreation (or re-creation), they can devote themselves to a relationship with You and Your service, unencumbered by the cares and folly of the world . Furthermore, some even feel that for them to show their love and devotion to You, Lord, they need even more space and silence and so choose a silent order or feel called to live out their vocation in solitude. In neither are they idle. Their very prayer and worship and the greater or lesser silence in which they live creates that space for them to immerse themselves more in You and Your Eternity. Then they can find their true inner beings and the relationship between You and the world. And in that silence they can pray for and intercede for our hurting world.

"Lamb of God, who takes away the sin of the world"[6], have mercy on us. That is surely the cry of all of us whether we have a vocation to silence, to live in a community or in the world. Help me, Lord, to learn from Your example and theirs how to live the Dance in Your silence.

[1] Psalm 87 v 7 Prayer Book Version 1662
[2] see Mark 1 v 35
[3] see Luke 3 v 22 & John 1 v 29 and of Isaiah 42 v 1
[4] Luke 4 vv 18 & 19 Authorised Version
[5] see Mark 6 vv 30-32 ; Luke 11 vv 1-4
[6] John 1 v 29

7.   PRIVATE PRAYER

Llanengan Church, LLyn Peninsula, North Wales, Margaret Doak

At Aylesford Priory near Maidstone, Kent
Agata Salawa-Adam

IN the Dance created by You, Lord Jesus, and those who feel called to serve You in a monastic setting, I see an example of how to set my own life in order and to live my life as You mean me to. I thank You for their lives and for those who are my fathers and mothers in the spiritual life and I seek a way in myself to replicate, even just a little, that space for silence and solitude in the midst of the busy-ness of my life. There are so many duties to be performed, so many letters to write, phone calls to make and receive, people to see besides and within the work I feel You have called me to do. I could so easily lose sight of You in the razzmatazz of daily life.

Is there a way through? I need You so badly to fill me afresh every day with Your living Presence, forgiveness and anointing by Your Holy Spirit. Therefore I must set aside a time when I can be alone with You to praise and worship You in the stillness and I ask that You will "Speak through the earthquake, wind and fire, O still small voice of calm!"[1] And that is what I need – calm in which to be able to live my daily life, to bring myself back into communion with You by confessing what is wrong, thanking You for salvation, for so many blessings and praying for the needs of ourselves and the world. I also need Your Word daily to give me a constant reminder of Your Love, example and encouragement.

Yet it could be so easy to leave my relationship with You there and forget You for the rest of the day – even though You don't forget me. So, Lord, please help me to use those spaces in the day when I am thinking of or doing nothing, when I am in a traffic jam, peeling the potatoes or drinking tea or coffee on my own. Help me to enter continually into that deep inner silence where I can let down all my masks, learn just to be and find You and my true identity, so that I may offer up myself and others to You to be recreated in Your image.

[1] From "Dear Lord and Father of Mankind"

V "MAN'S" USE OF NATURAL RESOURCES

1. FORESTRY

Barming Woods near Maidstone, Kent

Trees at Mlini near Dubrovnik on Croatian Coastline

FORESTS are wonderful, mysterious places to be in, Lord. There is that sense of otherness as one listens to the, sometimes eerie, sounds of animals and birds. There is something so alluring about such forests when the sun shines, so awesome when it is dark or raining, often with rain drops glistening on the tips of the branches. Indeed, "The trees of the Lord are well watered...There the birds make their nests; the stork has its home in the pine trees"[1]. They bespeak the majesty of Your Creation, and make me realise how small I am.

Your provision for us through forests has played an enormous role in our civilisation for which I thank You :charcoal and coal from trees that have decayed over the centuries;likewise their cork and wood for implements, houses and furniture. Forestation also attracts the rain that we need for our daily lives, crops and industry. You have so graciously provided for all our needs[2]. How sad it seems then, Lord, that there has not been a stricter ruling, until recently, for replanting trees that have been chopped down. So I perceive that the Sahara Desert, for example has grown ever larger because forestation has not been replaced and such mismanagement is causing drought, uncertain life, starvation. And many tribal communities, animals, birds and insects have been disrupted as a result of Government and industrial policies which have led to hurt, dislocation and loss of identity – even of life – for those concerned. Progress, I accept, is inevitable, but need it be at the exploitation of the land and its inhabitants? Could not "the Powers that be" find a more humane and caring way of dealing with the situation? If trees could talk they would have their own stories to tell. They have been silent witnesses of desecration and greed. Certainly I know that tribes-people like the Aboriginals do have controlled bush fires but I see that that is in order for the ground to be re-cultivated by the seeds which spring out as a result of the fire. They also treat their land as sacred as do other tribal units.

Heavenly Father, I see forest dwellers, whether human or all creatures of the universe singing their praises, unbeknown to them as maybe, of You and as part of the cosmic Dance in which all Creation tends towards a central point. Here too, I can join in. May we continue to be attracted to and uplifted by the virgin rain forests we still have and protect them.

[1] Psalm 104 vv 16 & 17

2. FARMING

Farming in Kent

FARMING I know to be the bedrock of our lives, for food of all descriptions – carbohydrates, protein, fruit and vegetables. I have great respect for farmers, Lord, who, like many others, are out in all weathers. Once, I gather that cultivation was more simple, if harsh work, and now highly sophisticated – at least in the West. Many are trying to produce goods organically again and rear free-range poultry, whilst others are testing out genetically modified products but I wonder, however if we should evolve such an order as this?

Here, farming can take many twists and turns – drought, blight, storms, prolonged snow, foot and mouth disease, T.B. The list could go on. I pray that we shall always treat farmers well and that they may be given due compensation when necessary. We owe our food to them. Yet, even so, sadly, how much harder it is for Third World countries who may experience all the same conditions as we do and even more so but earn only a pittance for their labour. Cocoa, rice, sugar, tea leaves are still harvested by family or child slave labour and in intense heat.At Harvest Festivals we may sing "The hills with joy are ringing, The valleys stand so thick with corn That even they are singing"[1]; and "All be safely gathered in, Ere the winter storms begin"[2]. I am deeply grateful for all the harvesting yet I know that so much depends on the weather and even human disasters.

Your Son, Lord, saw beyond the physical and material side of farming and related it to our spiritual lives in some of the most wonderful parables. Perhaps the best known is that intrinsic one about the Sower Who sowed seed – Your Word[3], on different types of soil but only one, the fertile soil, produced a good crop. I know that I need to ensure that I continually place my spirit in the good soil, over against the other kinds, where worry, riches and different interests – the interests of the world – can creep in, so that I can bear good fruit[4] before the final reaping[5]. And there is a note of urgency about all of these parables since Jesus saw that the crops were "ripe for harvest"[6] (the harvest of souls). Yet, there are ever too few to work, He said, to bring people into Your Kingdom and so continue the cosmic Dance. I pray that I and many workers may rise to the occasion so that all may receive Your Bread of Life and I thank You for those many who have given their lives to bring in Your Eternal Harvest throughout the world.

[1] From "To Thee, O Lord, Our Hearts We Raise"
[2] From "Come, Ye Thankful People, Come"
[3] see Mark 4 vv 1-20
[4] see Ibid and 2 Corinthians 9 v 6
[5] see Matthew 13 vv 24-30 & 36-43
[6] John 4 v 35

3.   FISHING

Fishing boats in Norway and Croatia

FISH seem to come in all sorts, sizes, shapes and colours, like humans. To see them swimming about in the sea, especially in the Barrier Reefs of the world, is to enter into a whole new sphere and we are still discovering different species. The variety which You have created, Lord, seems endless, causing people to be fascinated by them, even to keeping them as pets. Yet besides their sheer splendour there is that darker side that we have seen with mankind, of killing, disease, despoilation of the oceans and over-fishing.

How important the fishing industry has been throughout the ages can be gleaned from Your Son's life. We know that many of the Apostles were fishermen[1] and He told them that they would become fishers of men[2] -people who would preach Your Word and win souls for the Kingdom. He also showed how, just as fish were sorted into good and bad, so there would be a sorting at the end of the Age, of those who would belong to His Kingdom and those who would exclude themselves by rejecting the Good News[3]. Seemingly harsh but I see that we are given the means to accept, if we know about You, through Your Grace and the Salvation that Your Son procured for us. Then too, He fed the Five Thousand and the Four Thousand with Bread – symbolic of the Eucharistic Feast[4] – and fish. The Sea of Galilee, had so many different kinds of fish in it (153 we learn)[4] – a foreshadowing of the large variety of people of every race and culture who would be included in the Kingdom.

Abba, Father, thank You for providing sustenance for us in the form of fish and for their health benefits for us. And I thank You for those whose livelihood is fishing and for their endurance in harsh conditions at sea. Help me to appreciate fish for themselves as well as for their benefits for us and for their spiritual impact. How significant that the early Christians took the Greek word for fish – ICHTHUS (ΙΧΘΥΣ) – as a credal witness in times of persecution, using each letter as a word about Your Son – Jesus Christ God's Son, Saviour, 'Ιησους Χριστος Θεου Υίος, Σωτηρ'. So help me, Father, to be a strong witness in these days of indifference whilst for many in other parts of the world there is persecution.

[1] see Mark 1 vv 16-19 et al : John 21 vv 1-3
[2] see Luke 5 vv 1-11
[3] see Matthew 13 vv 40-51
[4] see Mark 6 vv 30-44 et al. Mark 8 vv 1-9 : John 21 vv 1-14

4. WOODWORK

Jim creating a Grandfather Clock and

repairing antique furniture

LORD JESUS, You hallowed the work of a carpenter by apparently working with Joseph, before Your Public Ministry. How many artefacts You must have made – furniture, beams for houses and synagogues, cradles, tools, yokes for cattle, coffins and even perhaps crosses. So it would seem that the very profession You were engaged in also became an instrument for Your Death.

We still need wood workers for many areas of life for although most articles are now made by machinery yet many people still like hand-made and turned wood-work and in parts of the world that is as yet the only way. I have seen some who are "skilled at the plane and the lathe"[1] handling wood and running their fingers gently over it, as You may have done and as if it were very precious. And such skill requires patience, endurance and precision to produce an object of quality much as a potter would work clay and remould it until it was perfect[2]. I see here too, a parable of how You work on me through the Holy Spirit, refining me till I am as You would have me be-and this work may well go on in Eternity. So I need to develop those same attributes as the wood workers – of patience to grow in Your Grace, endurance to persevere and precision rather than a careless attitude.

Dear Jesus, I am so blessed, for You said "Come to me, all you who are weary and burdened, and I will give you rest. Take my yoke upon you and learn from me....For my yoke is easy and my burden is light"[3]. How comforting to know that You, My Lord and Saviour, love me enough to give me a yoke that fits and is not difficult if I allow myself to follow in Your ways and example. In this way I can join in the Dance of Life and enter into Your Eternal Rest[4] which is Your Kingdom.

[1] From "Lord of All Hopefulness"
[2] see Jeremiah 18 vv 1-6
[3] Matthew 11 vv 28-31
[4] see Psalm 95 vv 8-11 and Hebrews 4 vv 1-11

5. ARCHITECTURE

St Mary's Fairfield, a Romney Marsh Church, Kent

Norman Church in Kent

Ely Cathedral, Cambridgeshire

Spanish Church Architecture

ABBA. FATHER, I perceive that architecture has been and is an expression of the need for buildings for domestic and commercial purposes and ecclesiastically for churches wherein to worship You, as Creator of the Universe. And there is an element of creativity which is continually evolving. Sometimes this is purely functional, at other times achieving something beautiful, grand, exotic or even unusual.

Furthermore what appears to be way out to some people, to others it has a special appeal. Fashion and ideas of the time have their part to play in the development of styles as well as of necessity.

I feel particularly aware of Church architecture and how it passed from being classical in style to a simple fortress-like building in Saxon times, also acting as a refuge from invaders. It seems that architects and designers forged ever onwards and upwards, the Normans embellishing and adding to the fortress kind of edifice, like Durham Cathedral, that they may have found. Later, I see that the Gothic style produced churches and cathedrals to aspire ever further heavenwards, making them, as it were, a paeon of praise to You. Such are Ely, Norwich and Salisbury Cathedrals. More modern approaches seem to have varied from somewhat mundane and purposeful to designs with a certain significance like the Roman Catholic Cathedral of Christ the King in Liverpool, which represents Your Son's crown of glory. Each has its own story to tell and to be sure, all of them must have been built with many risks and dangers involved, even to the collapse of scaffolding and causing workers to die as at Sens Cathedral in France in Medieval days.

Lord, I see herein a parable. My life appears to be like this. With the help of Your Grace and the Holy Spirit I am fashioning my own life. Sometimes I grow spiritually and at others I seem to go my own way. I know that I need to remain constantly in Your Grace and rely continually on Your Holy Spirit to enable me to keep my scaffolding in good repair, so that when I see danger signals I can trust in the framework of prayer and praise that I have been establishing. Ultimately I pray that I can continue that work of Grace which You have begun in me through the rites of initiation such as Baptism and Confirmation so that I may become a sweet smelling fragrance[1] as a witness to You in the world so that Your Kingdom may ever continue to grow.

[1] see Ephesians 5 v 2 ; Philippians 4 v 18

6.   WORK AND INDUSTRY

Embroiderers' Guild Market, Belgium

Office and town buildings, Maidstone, Kent

The tourist industry, Cavtat near Dubrovnik, Croatia

FROM the dawn of mankind work has been Your directive for us, Lord – first of all as stewards to care for and tend Your Creation[1], and then through disobedience to work by the sweat of our brow[2]. This is so often the case and much labour is still undertaken by sheer hard toil even with modern equipment and machinery. So many kinds of livelihoods are indeed unrewarding, humdrum, even perhaps backbreaking – road building and maintenance, building and repair work, re-building after earthquakes, storms and tempests to name but a few. Working in factories and salt mines, slave labour in many parts of the world, are physically and mentally exhausting. What we term industry – the manufacturing of many kinds of goods may be more interesting at the creative and inventive stage but the execution of it in the production line can be a boring time for so many and industrial and council estates seem to do little to alleviate or improve life after working hours with poor housing and social activities.

Fortunately however, for those at least who put their trust in You, the situation has been redeemed by Your Son so that what we do for a living can be undertaken as an offering to You for the good of us all and to enhance Your world. Yet this is still not the case for a large section of society nor for the world in general. I see that a few attempts have been made to reconcile this area of life as was the case in the Bournville village created by the Quakers two centuries ago on the outskirts of Birmingham, where workers were given houses in a pleasant environment with after hour social activities. Sadly more of this sort has not been achieved.

I realise Heavenly Father, how blessed I am. Though there may have been one or two less interesting moments in my life's work, for the most part it has been richly satisfying and rewarding. I am ever learning to place my life under Your direction, so that even the harder and duller aspects of it are performed as an offering to You for the betterment and enlargement of Your Kingdom. I pray that others may be equally enriched in their work.

[1] see Genesis 1 vv 26-28; 2 v 15
[2] see Genesis 3 v 19

74

7. CONSERVATION

Copse and wood near Maidstone, Kent   *Woodland scene, Mlini near Dubrovnik, Croatia*

"THE EARTH is the Lord's, and all that therein is"[1] and "The earth is filled with the fruit of thy works".[2] Indeed, Lord, You have created such a wonderful world for us to live in – seas and sky, mountains and hills, plains and valleys, rivers, forests and fresh air. "O Lord, how manifold are thy works;... the earth is full of thy riches"[3]. And You appointed us to be stewards of Your world, which would include planting, tending and watering it.[4] Where it is still cared for or there is a natural habitat, there continues to be beauty and I always feel re-created and refreshed when I am able to be in such places. I sense Your presence in a special way. What a privilege to be co-workers with You in caring for Your handiwork.

Sadly I see that industrialisation and urbanisation have often played havoc with our responsibility of stewardship. However, it is encouraging to know that in the second half of the last century and now in this century, important personalities like Prince Charles have taken such an active interest in awakening everyone's sense of duty towards preserving our environment. He and an increasing number of other people have activated many areas of improvement for farming, viably grown crops, natural surroundings and saving our coastline and hillsides, woodlands and forests. In Argentina, for example, Christians are making a real impact against deforestation. How thrilling to be involved in this aspect of stewardship. Isaiah foresaw a golden age when all nature would live in harmony under the leadership of a son of David – Your Son[5]. So too St Paul saw a time would come when the whole of Creation would be liberated and enjoy the same freedom as the children of God[6] and all living creatures would be renewed so that "The glorious Majesty of the Lord shall endure for ever: the Lord shall rejoice in his works"[7].

Heavenly Father, I want to be a good steward of Your Creation. Help me to start with my own home, recycling and so saving materials. I can make my garden a natural place for birds to come. I can also join schemes such as the National Trust and the Woodland Trust to conserve coastline, moors and forests, join in schemes to reclaim waste places and encourage more environmentally friendly regions of industrial output.

[1] Psalm 24 v 1 Book of Common Prayer 1662
[2] Psalm 104 v 13 ''
[3] Psalm 104 v 24 ''
[4] see Genesis 1 v 26; 2 v 15
[5] see Isaiah 11 vv 1-10
[6] see Romans 8 vv 18-22
[7] Psalm 104 v 31 Book of Common Prayer 1662

VI CREATIVE ACTIVITIES

1. ASTRONOMY

Mary, the Christ Child and Star,
Original Painting by Rosemary
Godfrey

David Darby

LORD, when I gaze into Your heavens at night, I am overwhelmed by the beauty and immensity of Your Creation, no matter where I am in the world. The position of the stars and planets may be different and there will be others according to where one lives. It just makes me realise how pertinent are Your words to Job; "Can you bind the beautiful Pleiades? Can you loose the cords of Orion? Can you bring forth the constellations in their seasons or lead out the Bear with its cubs? Do you know the laws of the heavens? Can you set up God's dominion over the earth?"[1].

Clearly, mankind has always been fascinated by the stars and planets and has gone far beyond wondering what they are as in "Twinkle, twinkle little star, how I wonder what you are". Astrologers from time immemorial have tried to tell people's fortunes, predict the future or fortuitous dates for weddings and other events. Yet the study of the stars by astronomers has more of the ring of truth. Eastern sages were led to Bethlehem to seek out Your Son at His Birth[2] and He is indeed "the bright Morning Star".[3] So what, I wonder, is it that is so alluring about the stars and planets that we have sought to find out how and what they are made of and if there has been or is life on the moon or planets? It certainly seems interesting and important to know the answers to these questions but I wonder if we are not in danger of attempting to play Your role, Lord, when we try to find out how and when the world was created by blasting two asteroids together ? You said that we must not eat of the tree of knowledge of good and evil[4]. Would it not be better to stop before we go too far?

Dear Father, "When I consider your heavens, the work of your fingers, the moon and the stars, which you have set in place, what is man that you are mindful of him?"[5] I see the stars and planets, some of them millions of years old, and other newer ones, as part of Your everlasting and continuous creative activity and it is sufficient for me to accept their presence as a welcome sign of their involvement in the Dance of Life of which You are the Author.

[1] Job 38 vv 31-33
[2] see Matthew 2 vv 1-12
[3] Revelation 22 v 16: see Numbers 24 v 17
[4] see Genesis 2 vv 15-17 & 3 vv 1-5
[5] Psalm 8 vv 3 & 4a

2.   ROCK AND CAVE ART

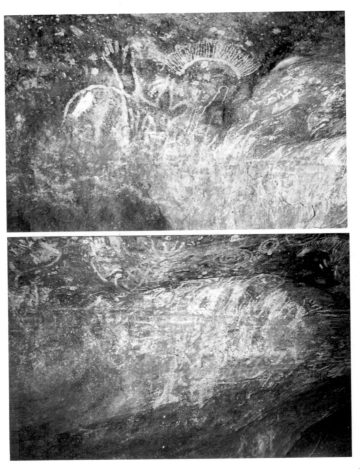

Cave paintings at Ayers Rock (Uluru) Northern Territories , Australia
Photographs by Margaret Doak

HEAVENLY Father, since Your Word has been active and You have communicated with us from the very inception of Creation, You clearly intended us to be social beings making contact with one another. I see that one way in which this happened was for cave dwellers and hunters the world over to draw, engrave, paint or stencil the walls of caves, depicting everyday events and their religious and spiritual life. There they would indicate where and how a triumph in hunting happened, where water was to be found, ritual war dances and symbols of their religious beliefs. It could also prove possession of a cave when the families or tribes involved would imprint their hands all over the cave walls by using coloured ochre powder and water on their hands. Some cave art is at least 50, 000 years old and it gives us an amazing picture of the life of the times. There are still some caves open for viewing and well preserved.

So here was a different way of life and culture which may now seem remote to us – and perhaps especially that of the Aboriginals in Australia – yet even if much has been lost, there remains enough for us to glean how these early peoples did communicate with each other and they have left their mark for their descendants. It would appear that their tribes spoke a variety of languages, so these paintings would have been one way in which they could all understand each other.

For me, Lord, to have seen rock and cave art first hand has a special significance. I felt a oneness with fellow human beings, whom though obviously I had never known, yet showed me how important the art of communication is for all of us to learn from and understand each other and which can either bind us together or sadly, tear us apart. Nevertheless such paintings as these paved the way for a developing "language" of communication which came to fulfilment in Jesus, Your Word. Grant, Lord, that my conversation with others may be welcoming, informative, reconciliatory where necessary and loving.

3. CHRISTIAN RELIGIOUS SYMBOLS

Loaves and Fishes Mosaic,Tabgha, Galilee, Israel
Margaret Doak

Elaborate Chi Rho rune in Franciscan Monastery, Island of Lopud,
Croatia

JUST as some people have drawn and painted in caves, Lord, from time immemorial, so too I see that others have depicted religious symbols. Christians also have derived their own images, frescoes and icons from various countries as well as from some of Your Son's miracles, parables, implements of His Passion and the saints. Again it seems as if this is all about communication. The five loaves and two fish so often found embedded in mosaics as at Tabgha in Galilee were thought of as signs that Jesus was the Messiah Who would feed His people mysteriously in the wilderness and early on were also seen as an indication of the Eucharistic feast.

The fish, it would appear, became a secret symbol to show that someone was a Christian during times of persecution and was a wonderful way of declaring one's faith privately as well as letting other Christians know that you too were a Christian. Ichthus, the Greek for fish was easily turned into a creed, each letter being the first one of each of the words "Jesus Christ God's Son, Saviour" (see chapter V. 3) Similarly the Chi Rho(XP in Greek) and variations thereof, were the first two letters of Christ (-the Messiah) – in Greek. Later, we know that the Celts here in the British Isles built up a whole host of symbolic images, especially circles, depicting the never-ending Eternal Life as part of the cosmic Dance.

Heavenly Father, though I would hope not to have to undergo persecution, I pray that even if the going is hard in an increasingly multi-faith and secular society, I will have the means whereby to show the world that I am a Christian believer, one of Your disciples and seeking to live in accordance with the Dance of life as taught by Your Son.

4. ART

The Somerset Levels

The River Exe at Exmouth, Devon
Original paintings by John Mair – our great uncle

ART seems to cover such a wide range of disciplines that it almost defies definition, Lord. I have always felt that Art should inspire us with beauty and be informative, such as the ones portrayed here. We have already reflected on two art forms, rock and cave art and Christian religious symbols. Other countries and continents too had many shapes and patterns, both secular and religious. I know that in the early days of Christianity most art was religious but over the centuries it has become less so here in the West. I have felt so enriched and empowered through the influence of Christian art with the images of Your Son, aspects of His Life, Death, Resurrection and Ascension as well as of the coming of the Holy Spirit and His saints, as paintings, icons and in stained glass windows. It seems as if they were the Gospel in pictures for those who could not read the Bible-in Latin or in one's mother tongue. The stories and the rich colours would have helped them, as they still do, to see the Good News as relevant and understand it.

The water colours and oil paintings of the Great Masters also inspire me, especially those of the idyllic scenes of the countryside. Such are often as influential as the purely Christian ones and frequently take me beyond myself. The Nineteenth and Twentieth Centuries saw further dramatic change. Artists seemed to be expected to be more creative and way-out, some becoming very abstract. Maybe the newer forms are

Devon Church
Original painting by Jim

there to inspire and inform and indeed some works presenting themes like warfare, tragedies, battles and killings are tremendously powerful.

Yet often it feels as if my head is in a fog where I can personally see no clear guide lines or information. It seems as if here art is saying that somehow we lost our way in the Twentieth Century.

Lord, amid the confusion and abstraction of so much of modern life, I ask that Your will may shine clearly before me as a guiding light to help me make sense of areas of life that seem to me to have no meaning currently. Help me to understand what the artists are trying to convey.

5. MUSIC

Marching band,
Cavtat, near Dubrovnik, Croatia

Musicians and Dancers at Sopron, Hungary, Photographs by Margaret
Doak

"IF MUSIC be the food of love, play on"[1]. So said the Duke of Illyria in Shakespeare's "Twelfth Night". Indeed, music can inspire that emotion in its many facets and I often feel quite overwhelmed – even transported – by the works of some composers, especially classical ones. I have been moved to deep emotions of love for You, Lord, for fellow human beings and a feeling of being in harmony with Nature and the whole world. I can feel encouraged to be creative, write, work or be full of joy and ecstasy. Yet at other times I can feel sorrowful for the state of the world according to the work of the composer. Sadly too, some more modern music seems to me to have a harsh, strident, even discordant note but that may be a true reflection of the state of current society.

Other forms of music have existed throughout the ages, each with their own appeal or otherwise. The psalms of David, still sung today (albeit with different tunes) and worship led by Levites and the orchestras of Biblical times were, it would appear, haunting, though we have lost many of the original melodies. Christian Church music throughout the ages has a very special place in my heart and can move me to worship and praise You and from early times there has been circle dancing which suggested the dancers dancing around Your Son, the Lord of the Dance. Music from other lands and traditions stir up differing emotions within me-there's the call of the wild, the call to celebrate or prepare for war in places like Aboriginal Australia, Papua New Guinea and Africa. Then there is the Swiss yodelling, folk songs, whether from Europe or America, India or Asia, the bagpipes from Scotland and Ireland, Gaelic, Irish and Welsh songs often with music played on the harp as were the Psalms, and Jazz as well as all the modern pop music which some will prefer to any other form.

Dear Lord, it is the rich variety I find in music and song which contributes to making life full of vitality and creativity. Help us to find that music which pleases us most, possessing no discordant notes but enabling us to live in harmony with You, the world and ourselves as I and each of us take our place in the Dance of Life.

[1] Act 1 Scene 1 line 1 "Twelfth Night" by Shakespeare

6.   TRAVEL BY LAND, SEA AND AIR

Gracious living, driving a Rolls Royce

North Yorkshire Railway

Norwegian Steamer

Aeroplane landing at Headcorn Aerodrome, Kent

IT appears that human beings have always been on the move, looking for new pastures, new beginnings, adventure and an inquisitiveness to know what is beyond the confines of the particular tribe, group or territory that people live in. Thus began travel overland using animals such as donkeys or camels. So too it appears that early man made simple boats, then more sophisticated ones over the centuries to ferret out what lands and riches there might be beyond their area, either by river or across the seas. Some territories had probably been connected by land before being split off and so peoples living in these places might well have set off to look for relatives as well as find new homes.

What toil and toll of life such cumbersome, and in earlier days, often flimsy boats there must have been when they "went out on the sea in ships;they were merchants on the mighty waters. They saw the works of the Lord, his wonderful deeds in the deep"[1], both in the tempests and the stilling of the storms[2]. How blessed then it feels today to be able to travel by a comfortable, even fast, car, bus or train, getting to one's destination either at speed on a motorway or by a slower route perhaps soaking up the beauty of the countryside. And how different from the days of coach and horses when it could take days to reach a given destination and perhaps be overwhelmed by highwaymen en route. Today too the world has shrunk to the size of a global village where passengers can travel from one end of the universe to the other in a matter of hours-in search once again of new homes, relatives or adventure-even work and interchange of goods and materials. Each mode of travel, I see Lord, has taken time, patience and skills to develop over the years and centuries and then learn to drive and control one's chosen means of voyaging.

No one who journeys by whatever means can fail to recognise that there are still inevitable dangers involved whether physical, mechanical or risk of hi-jacking or piracy. So dear Lord, whether I am in control or a passenger, may I learn to respect both the environment and other users of land, sea and air for the safety and enjoyment of all and to place my life in Your hands.

[1] Psalm 107 vv 23 & 24
[2] see ibid vv 26-33; Mark 4 vv 35-41 et al

7. LEISURE AND TOURISM

Pleasure Boats, Espoo, near Helsinki, Finland
Margaret Doak

Enjoying a market on holiday in Spain

Touring in Norway

Norwegian Pleasure Boats

"GOD blessed the seventh day and made it holy, because on it he rested from all the work of creating that he had done"[1]. Clearly, Lord, from the earliest days it was seen as necessary to have a day of rest-whether from the belief that You created the world in six days-or more accurately, from the Hebrew, in six eras or stages, or other motivation. For the Jews I see that it was not just a day of rest, but a period set aside to devote themselves to You in worship and praise. Sadly that day of rest, the Sabbath, became crowded with so many rules and regulations that they almost blotted out the original intention. Indeed, Your Son freed this holy day from the shackles of the Pharisaic Law and He restored it to its former glory when He said that "The Sabbath was made for man, not man for the Sabbath"[2] wherein 'man' was free to enjoy his relationship with You, and the blessings of Your Creation. Your Son was often to be found taking His disciples away from the crowds for refreshment, rest and teaching[3]. Nevertheless works of creation, mercy, justice, restoration and re-creation, and healing still needed to function on that day as well as worship[4].

So we see that the Biblical principle of "time off" was upheld by Your Son and the early Christians. Nowadays people have more freedom for leisure and holidays than ever before. Indeed holidays have passed from the "holy days" of worship and rest to the secular free time from work. How good it is to lay aside the busy-ness and stress of modern life, away from it all emotionally, physically, mentally and spiritually and be with family or friends or even go on a retreat. As travel has become easier, I see people seeking out further-flung and more remote places, which in turn have become popular and crowded.

I realise that some people like crowds but I believe, dear Lord, that it is of more benefit for my soul and spirit to be able to find a quiet spot in which to re-group and re-create whether in some far off place or in discovering such a place within myself, where I may once again pace my steps in tune with the Dance of Life.

[1] Genesis 2 v 3
[2] Mark 2 v 27 see Matthew 12 vv 7-8
[3] see Mark 6 vv 30-32
[4] see Luke 13 vv 10-16

VII "ALL CREATURES GREAT AND SMALL"

"All things bright and beautiful,
All creatures great and small,
All things wise and wonderful,
The Lord God made them all".

From "All Things Bright and Beautiful"

St Francis, lover of animals
Capuchin Monastery
Sintra near Lisbon, Portugal
Margaret Doak

INTRODUCTION

THE animals in this chapter all appear in the Bible and are mainly working ones but with one or two wild ones included. All have characteristics similar to our own and most play a part in human and Divine affairs.

NOTE: "CATTLE" in the Bible is a fairly general term which generally refers to and includes sheep; cows, bulls and oxen; camels; and donkeys or asses. They all seem to be in the forefront of a person's possessions and wealth and as the Patriarchs moved about so they would take all their cattle with them as well as their whole family and other possessions.

96

1. CATTLE

a) SHEEP

Highland sheep
Margaret Doak

Kentish sheep

HOW special sheep have been since time immemorial. The greatest names in the Old Testament from the dawn of mankind onwards, as also the monks of Medieval Europe, thrived on their wool trade and were considered rich, or not, according to the size of their flocks of sheep, to say nothing of their other animals. I see that sheep, Lord, were all important not just for their meat, milk and wool, but for sacrifice both in the days of the wilderness (and indeed, I recall that one saved the life of Isaac[1])and later in the Temple. They were thought to be pleasing to You, but with the passage of time You taught them that You preferred moral justice and sincerity to sacrifices offered by indolent, rich people[2], having had "enough of burnt offerings, of rams and the fat of fattened animals"[3]. What a thrilling moment in history when You chose humble shepherds guarding sheep, which were almost certainly being reared for Temple sacrifice on the hills around Bethlehem to be the first to see Your Son after His Birth[4] Yet little would they have realised how He was soon to fulfil and complete prophecy rather than popular expectations of deliverance from the Romans.

I know that ancient kingly rulers were often referred to as shepherds of their people but Israel's true Shepherd-King was Yourself[5]. Through Your Divine inspiration it was a thrill to find out that Your Son came in the figure of a Suffering Servant-a person or nation suffering on behalf of others and who would be "led like a lamb to the slaughter, and as a sheep before her shearers is silent"[6]. Of what immense significance for our salvation when Your Son fused the two roles, Himself being the Shepherd of His sheep[7] (people) and "the Lamb that was slain from the creation of the world"[8]. In Him we could find pasture, strength and safety yet at the same time He was the Shepherd Who chose to lay down His life voluntarily for the sake of His flock[9]. A once-for-all sacrifice in place of the continual offering of sheep and other animals[10].

Dear Heavenly Father, thank You for the role and humility of sheep and for Your Son's dual profession of Shepherd-King and Lamb, Victim for our redemption since " We all, like sheep, have gone astray".[11] No wonder we need a Shepherd to seek out the lost[12] and lay down His life for them. Please help me to acknowledge with gratitude the vocation that He undertook and live humbly so that I might share in the Dance of Life in Your Kingdom.

[1] see Genesis 22 vv 1-19
[2] see Isaiah 1 vv 10-17
[3] Ibid v 11b
[4] see Luke 2 vv 1-20
[5] see Psalm 80 v 1: Ezekiel 34
[6] Isaiah 53 v 7b
[7] see John 10 vv 1-20
[8] Revelation 13 v 8
[9] see [7] above and Mark 10 v 45
[10] see Hebrews 10 vv 3 & 14
[11] Isaiah 53 v 6
[12] see Luke 15 vv 1-10 & 13-32; John 10 vv 11 & 14

b) COWS, BULLS AND OXEN

Highland Cattle

New Forest Cattle
Photographs by Margaret Doak

LIKE sheep, I see Lord, that cows, bulls and oxen play a large part in our lives, giving us meat, milk and the use of their hides. It seems that some parts of the world view the cow as sacred although in western society this is not so. Nevertheless I see that their role has been significant in religious practice. First however, we note that cows featured in the dreams of the Pharaoh who imprisoned Joseph, yet whose intuitive listening to You, Lord, enabled him to prophesy seven years of plenty to be followed by seven years of famine[1]. I perceive that this was Your way of bringing good out of a bad situation for thus action could be taken and many lives saved, including Joseph's whole family[2].

Sadly however these animals were often portrayed as objects of pagan worship which infiltrated the worship meant for You-as in the case of the Golden Bull which Moses found that had been erected whilst he was talking with You on the mountain[3]. Cows and bulls are prominent throughout the Old Testament for the myriads of burnt and sin offerings made for various kinds of trespasses[4]. How could the blood of a cow or a bull atone for wrong doing, whatever the severity? The author of Hebrews saw that that was impossible[5]. By the time of the Prophets of the Eighth Century BC the best of the breed was being reared on rich pasture lands and the prophet Amos compared wealthy upper-class women with these cows as being pampered, overfed and overdressed[6]. Oxen, castrated bulls, were used for the most part for ploughing and the weight of their yoke made them stoop. No wonder Your Son said that His yokes was easy and His burden light[7] if we would accept it.

Cows, bulls and oxen, like sheep have many characteristics in common with human beings. Some are very obstinate-others are rebellious, like the Highland creature pictured here looks! Many are used in humble service in farming. Apparently in some countries, to have eyes like those of a cow means that they are kindly and gentle. It seems that here we have a summary of what the human race can be like-obstinate, rebellious[8], yet also even hard working, kindly and gentle.

Dear Lord, help me to respect the contribution of these animals to my life and I pray that they may receive humane and caring treatment. Seeing so many farmers on the television makes me realise that most of them do care and make use of veterinary developments for their welfare.

[1] see Genesis 41
[2] see Genesis 42-47
[3] see Exodus 32
[4] see Leviticus 1 ; 4 et al
[5] see Hebrews 9 vv 11-15
[6] see Amos 4 v 1
[7] see Matthew 11 vv 28 & 29
[8] see Isaiah 1 vv 2-4

c)   CAMELS

Camels resting at Jericho
Margaret Doak

CAMELS were the transport animals of the Ancient Near East. So incredibly strong were they and able to store water in their stomachs it appears that they were able to go for long periods in the desert. We know that both of these things were important assets to a nomadic people. They were also used in farming and their hair was tough and so used for clothing[1]. An impressive list of gifts, Lord, which obviously added to a man's wealth. How many interesting stories occur in the Bible concerning these animals[2]. Camel trains would have been a familiar sight trekking across the desert and certainly they were in use by the time of Abraham, if not earlier. He transported them around the Fertile Crescent to Palestine[3] and also sent camels with his servant to find a wife for Isaac. Rachel answered the servant's prayer by offering to water his camels[4]. We have indeed to be grateful to camels for covering vast distances for trade and bearing goods of all kinds like silks, spices, perfumes and precious stones, purple and ivory along the silk-routes of the Ancient Near East from as far as India and Persia[5]. Yet, how blessed we are that modern transport means that all our materials arrive at their destination much more quickly! Later on, the Wise Men would almost certainly have travelled to find the Saviour of the world by camel and John the Baptist, we learn, wore a garment of camel's hair.[1] Your Son said that it was easier for a camel to go through the eye of a needle than a rich man to enter the Kingdom of Heaven[6]. I appreciate that the camel being the largest animal in Palestine contrasted teasingly with the smallest gate in Jerusalem called "The Eye of a Needle" and shows that our attempts to enter the Kingdom are useless without Your grace.

In our modern world camels still feature for riding and even carrying burdens. Nomads in Israel still use these lordly creatures to travel in the desert. They are also to be found in countries like Australia where they were transported from Afghanistan whose mountainous territory makes them ideal for moving around. Riding on one is rather bumpy and they have a habit of spitting and being grumpy. No wonder if they are ridden by an inexperienced person!

Once again dear Lord, I see an animal used in the service of mankind. I do pray that as stewards of the earth we may appreciate and treat them humanely. And I see in camels characteristics with which humans can identify and learn from. They may well have reason to be grumpy. So may we at times, but I hope that if I feel so inclined I may be able to curb it and turn my desire to be that way over to You. Rather, let me sing Your praises since I have so much to thank You for and to pray for those whose lives are less rich than mine.

[1] see Mark 1 v 6
[2] see Genesis 31 v 34: 1 Kings 10 v 2 et al
[3] see Genesis 12 v 16
[4] see Genesis 24 especially vv 10-31
[5] see 1 Kings 10 vv 2
[6] see Mark 10 vv 24-25

d) DONKEYS / ASSES

Donkeys at work on the beach

Photographs by Agata Salawa-Adam

DONKEYS too take their place amongst the cattle who were accounted as part of a man's wealth and have been much used in the service of mankind as burden-bearers and in farming also from the time of Abraham onwards[1]. So often, Lord, I have heard someone called "silly ass", suggesting the stupidity of these creatures, yet two outstanding stories point to the opposite. First, there was Balaam, a false prophet who wanted the money that Balak, son of the king of the Israelites' enemies, the Moabites, offered him. It was however, a dumb donkey that rebuked Balaam for his folly[2]. An interesting story maybe, but shows human weakness and that such an animal was not as stupid as has often been made out to be.

This story is corroborated by Your Son Who rode on a donkey into Jerusalem just a week before His death, rather than on a horse[3]. I see that He was pinpointing the fact that He was no warrior-king who would fight against the Romans, but rather as Zechariah had foretold, that Israel's King would come as "gentle and riding on a donkey"[4]- our Saviour Who would do away with war-horses and proclaim peace to the nations. Clearly He saw that donkeys were the epitome of gentleness, meekness and peace. Though some may still have been wild, the one Your Son rode on obviously belonged to a man living in Jerusalem who intended to break this donkey in and use it for domestic purposes. Furthermore it appears that a donkey which had not been ridden was considered suitable for religious purposes. And the fact that He was able to ride an unbroken colt is a wonderful indication not just of peace on earth but of His Reign where humans and animals would live in harmony[5]. Tradition also has it that Mary rode on a donkey when fleeing to Egypt with Joseph and Jesus. Sadly however, I note that donkeys, in common with many an animal, are so often maltreated, overworked, underfed and neglected-health-wise and yet they still perform the quiet, humble service of burden-bearing in many parts of the world, give children rides on the beach and children with disabilities a new outlook on life by riding on them. Many who are illtreated are however rescued, thankfully, by the Elizabeth Svendsen Trust.

Heavenly Father, what a wonderful place the donkey holds in our Salvation-History – a humble, meek and gentle creature chosen by Your Son in fulfilment of prophecy[4] for His final earthly entry to Jerusalem, yet all too often despised. Nevertheless, may I imitate these characteristics portrayed by donkeys and be amongst those who are the burden bearers, the meek who will "inherit the earth", the peacemakers who will be called "the sons of God"[6] and keep my silence until I know for certain what You want me to say.

[1] see Genesis 12 v 16
[2] see Numbers 22-25 & 31 vv 8 & 16
[3] see Luke 19 vv 28-38
[4] Zechariah 9 vv 9-10
[5] see Isaiah 11 vv 1-10
[6] see Matthew 5 vv 5 & 9

2. HORSES

Austrian Cart Horses

New Forest Horse

Lipica Riding School in Slovenia
Photographs by Margaret Doak

LIKE camels, I note that horses have been used throughout the ages for their size and strength and have been used in farming but more especially in warfare right up until modern times. So strong are they that they need bits and bridles[1]. The Bible tells us that they were ridden by the Egyptians who chased the fleeing Israelites to the Red Sea and were drowned[2]. And so began the Salvation-History of the Israelites who sang "The horse and its rider" the Lord has "hurled into the sea. The Lord is my strength and my song; he has become my salvation"[3]. No wonder, Lord, that Moses, Your servant, saw that future leaders and kings of Israel should be forbidden to possess large numbers of horses for themselves and should not make the Israelites go back to Egypt to accumulate more horses – and perhaps be re-enslaved there[4]. Sadly however, it appears that kings did acquire large numbers for warfare throughout their history[5].

On occasions You revealed Your heavenly hosts as angels or, as in the case of Elijah's departure from earth, by chariots and horses of fire[6]. Whatever the background of this event, it seems to prove that You had been with Elijah throughout his ministry and supported him, showing that he was the true strength of the nation not that of horse power and warfare. And what a wonderful depiction of the future peace that Your Son came to bring when He rode into Jerusalem on a donkey and not on a horse[7].

Dear Lord, I see that the Psalmist said that Your "pleasure is not in the strength of the horse", but rather You delight "in those who fear" You and "put their hope" in Your "unfailing love"[8]. Sad to say that horses have all too often been used in warfare and also been maltreated by many owners. How much better their use in domestic and civil purposes and farming, as often still in many parts of the world, especially if they are well cared for. As I study their characteristics I see that they are not just powerful but also devoted servants of mankind and I pray that I too may be as strong and faithful a servant of Yourself.

[1] see Psalm 32 v 9
[2] see Exodus 14
[3] Exodus 15 vv 1b & 2
[4] see Deuteronomy 17 v 16
[5] see 1 Kings 4 v 26
[6] see 2 Kings 2 vv 1-18
[7] see Luke 19 vv 28-38 et al; and see previous section
[8] Psalm 147 vv 10 & 11

3. DOGS

Two of Jim's dogs – Archie and Heidi

TODAY, dogs are kept largely as pets though there are a variety of working dogs – guard dogs, farm and sheep dogs, sniffer dogs, guide dogs for the blind, "hearing" dogs, sledge-pulling dogs to name but a few. We are supposed to be an animal-loving nation here in Britain, Lord, but it seems that there is much cruelty towards these – as to other creatures – hence the work of the R.S.P.C.A. And a plethora of other animal charities.

Certainly there were guard dogs in Israel both for one's house [1] and for protecting sheep from wolves and hirelings[2]. And I am sure that little dogs were kept as household pets[3] but for the most part it seems that they wandered around in large numbers or packs, rather like wolves, who preyed on dead bodies. Such was the case of the wicked and hated Jezebel, the wife of King Ahab, about whom it was prophesied "Dogs will devour Jezebel by the wall of Jezreel" And also "dogs will eat those belonging to Ahab who die in the city"[4]. They were fierce and disliked so much that I see that one's enemies were often referred to as "dogs" as a term of contempt[5]. Being an unclean animal, the word "dog "was often also used as a term of reproach about oneself or others[6]. However, on a happier note, in Your Son's time it certainly seems clear that dogs were kept as pets – a reference to which was made by the Syro-Phoenician woman who begged Him to heal her daughter. Although it was His mission to tend "the lost sheep of the house of Israel", this dear lady was prepared to settle for a crumb of His mercy like the crumbs thrown to the little dogs, as the Greek implies, under the table[3].

So dear Lord, although I see that there are still many cruel actions concerning dogs, yet it is good to know that they do have a much better status on the whole today than in Old Testament times. I pray that we may indeed learn to treat them all as Your Son and St Francis would have done. I know that I have much to learn from dogs. They are faithful, trusting and loyal, usually wanting to please their owners. Working dogs are employed for their ability to learn skills, be obedient and get on with the task in hand. Here I see characteristics that as a Christian You would want me to have.

[1] see Isaiah 56 v 10
[2] see Job 30 v 1
[3] see Matthew 15 vv 21-28 esp vv 26-27
[4] 1 Kings 21 especially vv 23 & 24
[5] see Psalm 22 v 16
[6] see 1 Samuel 24 v 14: 2 Samuel 16 v 9

4. LIONS

Photographs by Graham Osborn

LIONS roamed the ancient world in packs as today in the jungle. The name seems to have once again been synonymous with strength, so strong are they. They were obviously very common because there are so many references to and stories about them in the Bible and especially of their ferociousness, killing people and tearing at their carcases[1]. I see this, Lord, like with other wild animals, as a sign of a fallen world, and I know that the law of the jungle still exists where "The lions roar for their prey"[2]. And history tells us that early Christians were thrown to the lions for food, torture and sport. Lions also often appear in apocalyptic literature, art and architecture as a symbol of their strength.

There is, however, I note, another and more positive, hopeful side to lions which foresees the promise of a Creation which will be transfigured. Isaiah looked forward to a time when wild animals like the lion would be tame and would mingle freely with human beings-a prophetic overview of the time when You and Your Son's Kingly Rule would be established[3]. I see a glimpse of this gentler side of lions in the story of that saintly figure, Daniel, who refused to acknowledge the so-called god-like power of king Darius, the Mede, over against Your Majesty. You rewarded Daniel's faithfulness and vindicated him when You shut the mouths of lions to whom he was thrown for they apparently recognised Your authority despite their hunger[4]. Such was Your way of spreading Your dominion. Then when Your Son went into the desert prior to beginning His public ministry to fast and pray, we are told that He was there with wild animals. These would certainly have included lions. Yet His holy, untainted character protected Him from them – Isaiah's words, inspired by You being fulfilled in the One Perfect Person the world has ever known and lived. Furthermore as Your followers obey Your commands so we see Your Kingdom dawning. We learn that St Jerome was able to pull a thorn out of a lion's claw...People like the Adamsons in "Born Free" and "Living Free" did much work with lions in trying to tame them though sadly we know that Joy was eventually savaged by one, showing that as St Paul said, we are still striving for Your Creation to be liberated from the effects of sin[5].

Heavenly Father, Your Son was referred to as "the Lion of the tribe of Judah"[6] the strong yet meek Saviour. And once again, I see that there are characteristics in lions that are good and that we can imitate, when they are tamed. Such is the case with their strength. You need disciples who are strong and can resist the devil who prowls around as a roaring, untamed, lion seeking someone to tear apart from faith in You[7]. Help me too, to temper strength with gentleness and to recognise Your authority over my life.

[1] see 1 Kings 13 vv 23-26; Nahum 2 v 12
[2] Psalm 104 v 21
[3] see Isaiah 11 vv 1-10 especially vv 6-9
[4] see Daniel 6 especially vv 16-28
[5] see Romans 8 vv 13-25
[6] Revelation 5 v 5
[7] see 1 Peter 5 v 8

CONCLUSION

ANIMALS IN THE SCHEME OF SALVATION – HISTORY

Here are just a few of them!

Croatian cat

Zebra and giraffes at Longleat, Wiltshire
Photographs by Margaret Doak

Tigers enjoying a roar
Graham Osborn

Abyssinian Monkey
Terry and Valerie Oliver

Black swan and ducks at Leeds
Castle near Maidstone, Kent

IN this chapter we have looked at the lives and work of just a few animals – some more clearly involved in our religious lives than others but all with characteristics from which we can learn or imitate. All animals deserve humane treatment for all are creatures of our God. All have shared in what we term as the Fall of Mankind, but through the work of Christ we look forward to that time of transfiguration when His Kingly Rule will be established over all Creation everywhere[1]. In the meantime, Jesus said that "the kingdom of God is within you"[2] -His Kingdom can grow and be nurtured in us here and now while we await the final declaration of it and receive the full benefits thereof. We do not know the final destiny of animals nor should it worry us, but it is quite clear that God intended us, created as we are in His image, to be stewards of His World (not vindictive rulers) and have due care and respect for all His Creation as participators in His rule[3]. Only thus can we fully enter into the Dance of Life and be in tune with our Creator.

[1] see Isaiah 11 vv 1-10
[2] Luke 17 v 21
[3] see Genesis 1 vv 26 & 28; 2 v 15; Psalm 8 vv 6-8

EPILOGUE

TO THINK THROUGH

I a) How do you view Creation? Do you see it as an act of God, chance or totally incomprehensible? Is there an alternative way of answering the question? If so how would you answer it?

b) How do you see the elements involved in the Dance of Life? How far do you think they are dancing in tune with the Creator? If not, how and why not?

II a) In what ways do you see the hand of the Creator in Nature, or is it mere chance that the coast, mountains, hills, valleys and plains, rivers and islands have been formed as they are?

What causes change and why?

b) Can it be said that Nature reflects the glory of the Creator? If so, how does this happen?

III a) How has the "greenhouse" dilemma affected the seasons and climate? Do you see these changes as all "man's" fault or is there another dimension at work but which might, or not, include mankind?

b) Jesus said that earthquakes and famines were the beginnings of the birth pangs and sufferings before the "end of the age". How does this relate to today? Why do you think that we have not been told when the end will come?

IV a) The Bible and Christian teaching are full of prayer and worship and clearly expect Christians and believers in God to practise both. In what ways do you feel 1) drawn to prayer, 2) the need to pray and worship, 3) the need of aids to help you? How important is prayer, worship and the Eucharist to you and why?

b) How can prayer enhance our relationship with God? Why should God want our prayer and worship and how is it that it can effect change?

V a) In what ways do you see "man's" use of natural resources interacting with 1) the Creator 2) Creation?

b) How far are "man's" use of natural resources in tune with those of the Creator? Do you see any areas which are harmful to society? If so which ones are and why? Are there other natural resources that could be or are used?

VI a) How can creative activities such as astronomy and various forms of art and music enable us to understand more of Creation and our surroundings?

b) What other creative activities can lead to the fulfilment of "man's" potential and his reaching out to what is beyond him?Should we try to discover the moment of Creation?

If so, why? If not, why not?

VII a) What is the role of animals in Creation and in our daily lives? Some creatures seem less desirable than others even if they have uses. What should be the Christian attitude to them?

b) Why do you think that human beings are often so cruel to animals? Is there a connection between cruelty to them and to humans? Where does such cruelty come from? Why do you think that some people are vegetarian (apart from a dislike of meat!) ?

Conclusion: How do you view the Dance of Life and do you feel a part of it? If so, how;if not, why?